Reflections

Robert Brault

<>‹›<>

Also By Robert Brault

Round Up The Usual Subjects

The Second Collection

Thoughts on Art & Artists

*Short Thoughts For The Long Haul
(Anthology Selection)*

~~~

<>‹›<>

Again, for Joan

*"He was a sad and lonesome clown,
And she was the circus that came to town."*

~~~

<>< ><>

Created and published using the Amazon KDP Independent Publishing Platform.

This book may be purchased on Amazon sites worldwide or directly from the author at rbrault.blogspot.com.

ISBN-13:   978-1548019365

Front cover: "Fall Pond", watercolor by Joan Brault

<>< ><>

<><><>

Author's Note

I want to underscore the fact that all writings in this book are original.

Some may ring familiar, having appeared on the internet and in media outlets around the world.

It is difficult to protect one's creative rights to short writings such as these, and I am accustomed to seeing my thoughts credited to others, often to the famous. My books are a hopeful attempt to lay claim to the major part of my work. That said, I do encourage the free use of my items for non-commercial purposes, asking only attribution. I expect commercial users to contact me for permission.

Robert Brault

bobbrault@att.net
rbrault.blogspot.com

<><><>

Contents

<><><>

~~~

Perhaps an optimistic faith is a rosy interpretation of the facts -- or perhaps an optimistic faith is a factual interpretation of the rose.

~~~

<><><>

<>‹›‹›

Preface

   With this, the third and final collection of my thoughts and observations, I add to the literary world's sizable collection of "slim volumes." It turns out to be an opus of 144 pages.

   Will this indeed be the final volume? Yes, I think so. For once, and at long last, there is nothing more in the hopper, and a glance up the assembly line shows little more on the way. That is why I have chosen to publish now, and to publish what little I have -- to tie a ribbon around the whole lifetime effort, so to speak.

   I offer *Reflections* as a supplement to my other pocket-size volumes, *Round Up The Usual Subjects* and *The Second Collection*. Taken together, the three comprise pretty much the whole nine yards of my internet postings and earlier magazine writings.

   In *Reflections*, readers of my previous books will recognize the usual range of topics and the usual blend of the serious and the light-hearted. I can best characterize the collection, I think, by repeating the words of my original preface to *Round Up The Usual Subjects*. They remain an apt description.

<>‹›‹›

<><><>

"The thoughts, for the most part, are geared to tried and true virtues -- to faith, hope and charity, to pluck and optimism, to tolerance, compassion and understanding. Mixed in, you will find a healthy dollop of the wry, the sly and the facetious, but you find no malice.

"Will you find wisdom in these pages? Yes, but only the wisdom you bring to them. My goal is to put into words that which we all know full well but seldom express. The deal, as I tell my blog readers, is that I supply the words, you supply the insight."

That said, I hope you enjoy the book.

Robert Brault
September 2019

<><><>

Acknowledgments

My thanks to Terri Guillemets, founder of *The Quote Garden* (quotegarden.com) whose sponsorship of my internet blog was a key factor in its success.

Thanks also to my blog readers, especially to those who regularly left comments or sent encouraging emails. You know who you are (and so do I.)

And deepest thanks to Joan Brault, my wife, partner and soul mate, whose artwork graces the cover of this book and whose loving support graces my life.

~~~

<><><>

<>‹>‹>

~~~

No matter what you accomplish in life, a part of you still sits at a curbside, still hearing the drumbeat of a distant parade, still waiting for it to turn the corner.

~~~

<>‹>‹>

<>‹›<>

Achievement

Keynote Thought

There is no limit to what one person can do, and, fortunately, that is who most of us are.

Observations

It is a worthy achievement to raise oneself above the average but a worthier achievement to raise the average.

~~~

A watershed moment in life is the day you realize that what you can or can't do is a test of your resolve, not an extrapolation of your resume.

~~~

The danger in life is that we will choose to do nothing because we know how, choose to go nowhere because we know the way.

<>‹›<>

<> <> <>

Achievement

The Voice Of Experience

If you spend your life waiting for a chance, you are spending your chance waiting.

~~~

You learn this -- that if you're ever going to take on a challenge, you're going to take it on before you're ready.

~~~

The first requirement in taking a step in the right direction is to take a step in some direction.

If You Want My Advice

Before you recite the reasons why you can't, try to imagine them as the reasons why you didn't.

~~~

Never be discouraged by people who don't know what you're about to accomplish.

<> <> <>

Pushing On Regardless

Sometimes you feel like giving up, but then you look at other people who have given up, and you realize that the results aren't that good.

~~~

Often in life you have to fail small to achieve large.

~~~

Never mind that your actions seem hopeless. Act nevertheless, for you have a greater ability to act than to judge hopelessness.

Just Curious

If you don't dare to disturb the status quo, then what exactly do you plan to disturb?

<><><>

<><><>

Aging

Keynote Thought

From a diary: "Turning 80 this year. First time ever for me. Will be new at it and will doubtless make beginner mistakes. But looking forward to the opportunity."

Observations

Growing old together is a stage where two people who could never part without a kiss never part and so never kiss.

~~~

If you wonder why older couples do not more often hug and kiss, you do not appreciate the intimacy of just growing old together.

~~~

One of life's regrets is how few goodbyes you say compared to the number of people you never see again.

<><><>

One thing you learn in life is that if you're going to celebrate, celebrate as soon as possible.

~~~

Aging is a process by which, one by one, the trophies on your mantel are replaced by pictures of the grandkids.

~~~

If all you want in life is to be left alone, then time is on your side.

~~~

It is a mercy that the things we do in our youth to ruin our lives have so little youth to work with.

Speaking For Myself

I don't claim to know it all, but the older I get, the less I have to hear to know the rest.

~~~

To grow old with a loving companion is to outlive all your regrets.

Animals

Keynote Thought

There are times when I need the company of people -- and other times when I need the company of creatures who were never expelled from paradise for wanting to become God.

Observations

If animal intelligence were scored like figure skating, human beings would have the high score that is thrown out.

~~~

Human beings are the only animal you can torture, and no one will say, "They actually like that."

A Whimsy

I dreamed it was the end of the world, and I ran into two dogs talking, and one said, "Oh, we thought you had all left."

<>< ><>

Apology

Keynote Thought

An apology is an obligation without a due date. If owed, it is due. If due, it is overdue.

Observations

So often an apology is a letter written but never mailed, or, in the modern era, something you delete from your DRAFT folder a month later.

~ ~ ~

Actually you can change the past. There are many ways to do it -- by apology, by atonement, by admission, and that's just the a's.

~ ~ ~

A sure way to end up friendless in life is to outlive the person who was doing all your apologizing for you.

<>< ><>

Attitude

You can live the same life happily, feeling blessed, or unhappily, feeling entitled.

Observations

It is just too fundamental to happiness -- a positive attitude -- to let it depend on the last thing to happen to you.

~~~

The trouble with reacting to slights and snubs is not that it magnifies trivial things but that it enlarges small people.

~~~

There is nothing so apt to be returned to you in kind as your attitude toward another person.

<><><>

<>＜><>

Beauty

Keynote Thought

The eternal war -- nature's attempt to make every woman beautiful, society's insistence that she remain young and pretty.

Observations

The problem with disguising one's age to preserve one's youth is that one's age is so often better looking.

~~~

It can take a keen eye to see the beauty hidden beneath the layers of trying to look young.

~~~

Eventually you realize that you have pretty much the face your mom warned you might freeze that way if you weren't careful.

<>＜><>

<>< ><>

Being Yourself

Keynote Thought

If God had wanted a better you, He would have created a better you. And that's the challenge -- He did.

Observations

The surest way to become the person you were meant to be is to take it upon yourself to mean it.

~~~

It is unlikely that any of us was born to find out what someone else would do in our shoes.

~~~

There is nothing so given to a leap of progress as the task of becoming your true self. Where is the law that says you must begin today where you left off yesterday?

~~~

It is the worst trade we make in life -- who we are for what we want.

<>< ><>

One reason to become the person you were meant to be is so that someone else might have the friend they were meant to have.

Dry, Sly and Wry

The real you -- someone you briefly were before common sense prevailed.

~~~

There are times when you wish you could be someone else, a feeling quickly cured by getting specific.

~~~

Generally it's better to be a first-rate you than a second-rate someone else, even if it means taking a pay cut.

~~~

Never mind what the world expects of you. It is too low a standard to be concerned about.

<><><>

Belief

The mind is an exclusive club, a new belief only admitted on the thumbs-up of a present member.

Observations

Often there are words you'd be ready to believe again, if only someone would say them again.

~~~

If people want to believe, the facts won't stop them, and if they don't want to believe, the facts won't make them.

~~~

It is one thing to have made up your mind, and another thing to have made up your eyes and ears.

~~~

<u>What-If</u>: What if you opened a line of communication between the thinking part of your brain and the believing part of your brain?

<><><>

<>‹›‹›

Caring

<u>Keynote Thought</u>

*What can one person do? One person can prove
false the notion that nobody cares.*

<u>Observations</u>

*You can be a caring person or nobody's fool. It is a
difficult thing to be both.*

~~~

*The trouble with caring only about yourself is that
it invariably leads to not caring about anyone.*

<u>Words, Looking Back</u>

*Though battered by daring,
Not sorry I dared.
Thought sorrowed by caring,
Not sorry I cared.*

<><><>

Civility

I nod to a stranger, and the stranger nods back, and two people go off feeling a little less anonymous.

Observations

In an age when manners and civility have gone the way of dressing for dinner, you begin to understand why people dressed for dinner.

~~~

You can't please everyone, but you can usually please people who say please.

~~~

The principal social grace is to just find the other person interesting.

~~~

I recall a different time, when a moment of civility did not catch you so completely by surprise.

<><><>

It is probably a mistake to think that you can be selectively uncivil.

Appreciation

Perhaps you cannot make another person's thankless task less difficult, but you can always make it less thankless.

~~~

Some people can read minds or interpret body language -- but most people need to be told they're appreciated.

~~~

Never suppose that someone knows they're appreciated unless you can recall specifically the mechanism by which they would know.

Overheard at a Cocktail Party

"I don't quite remember who you are, but I remember being delighted to meet you."

<><><>

<><><>

Commitment

Keynote Thought

They who lack the energy for commitment greatly underestimate commitment as a source of energy.

Observations

On the one hand, don't take everything personally. On the other hand, don't expect anything to change until you do.

~~~

A question to occasionally ask yourself is this, "What did I approve today by remaining silent?"

~~~

Speaking For Myself

Do I miss, in a committed life, the freedom to choose? Not as much as I would miss the freedom I feel, having made my choice.

<><><>

<><><>

Cosmic Understanding

Keynote Thought

The first step to finding the one answer is to see it all as one mystery.

Observations

A scientist's belief in dark matter, dark energy and dark flow only proves that it's hard to explain the universe without reference to a mystical, unseen Trinity.

~~~

All it takes is one person who cares, and it is no longer a vast, uncaring universe.

~~~

If you understand compound interest, you basically understand the universe.

<><><>

<><><>

Cosmic Understanding

Personal Musings

I am a mortal being, microscopic in size compared to the vast, timeless universe. If I am to be happy, or, indeed, if I am to be sad , then it goes without saying that I must blow things out of proportion.

~~~

I had this dream where I said to God, "Why did you create the world?" and God said, "Actually, that wasn't me."

~~~

Being a little hard-of-hearing, I always get briefly excited when I hear that astronomers have discovered a new consolation.

Words, Looking Up

Another night, another "Why?"
I launch into the starry sky
To echo as a fading sigh
Across the reach of no reply.

<><><>

Couples

Keynote Thought

I saw by the duckpond an elderly couple,
throwing crumbs on the water,
thinking each other's thoughts,
casting each other's shadow,
and I wondered which had been the great love
and which the acquired taste
that became an addiction.

Observation

There are couples a matchmaker would match every
time, and couples who, for no rhyme or reason,
rhyme.

Overheard at a 60th Wedding Anniversary

"They told us it could only end badly, so we decided
not to let it end."

<><><>

Courage

Keynote Thought

It is an extraordinary courage that responds not merely to the moment but shows up each day for another 12-hour shift.

Observations

No one is born a hero, which is why when one of us performs an act of heroism, there's a parade down Main Street.

~~~

The hero and the coward have this in common -- that each thinks they did what anyone else would have done.

~~~

If there is a lesson to take from the Great Pandemic, it is to acknowledge more often a passing stranger -- on the chance that he or she might be a hero.

<><><>

Speaking For Myself

I never hear the phrase, "quiet courage" without appreciating how much of any human virtue lies in its quietness.

~~~

To see vulnerability hiding behind a brave face is to wonder if there is really anything more attractive in a human being.

~~~

One thing I have come to admire in my older years is the quiet courage of those who have stood at the graveside of their only consolation.

~~~

<><><>

<><><>

The Daily Grind

There is no actual law that says you can't get locked into a daily routine that makes you happy.

Observations

It would be instructive if occasionally we could see past the aggravation of the daily commute and appreciate the hope in it.

~~~

A question to ask yourself each morning is what you would do if you had today to live over again.

~~~

The measure of any day is what you get done while you're wondering if there's any use doing it.

<><><>

<><><>

The Daily Grind

It's hard, sometimes, to remember that you woke up just a few hours ago with no intention of antagonizing anyone.

~~~

The reason they define it as twenty-four hours is so that you'll know when to call it a day.

The Voice of Experience

No matter how you rush about, you never reach a moment in time ahead of anyone else.

~~~

Whatever you're trying to prove, it's good to occasionally spend a day not trying to prove it.

~~~

More important than how your day goes is having someone in your life to ask how it went.

<><><>

<><><>

Speaking For Myself

Looking back on my life, I was always prepared for the day I would meet my Maker but could have been better prepared for the days I didn't.

If You Want My Advice

Never let anything ruin your day that is not on the list of things you will let ruin your day.

~~~

Never postpone taking a vacation thinking you won't get another chance to postpone taking a vacation.

The Workplace

Workplace Rule #1: "The job of a manager is to identify the 20% of the people who do 80% of the work, and get them to do it all."

~~~

The basic premise of corporate downsizing is that if a job is being done right, the person doing it is unnecessary.

<><><>

Ever wonder what you might achieve if climbing the management ladder and managing something were the same skill?

~~~

A toast today to all the invisible people doing the jobs that magically do themselves.

Dry, Sly and Wry

One indication that you're meant for a higher calling is that you can't get hired for any of the lower ones.

~~~

There are days when you feel that if you walked down the street in a clown costume, no one would recall seeing anyone in a clown costume.

<>< ><>

<><><>

Destiny

Keynote Thought

We can usually recognize the consequences of our actions. It is the consequence of our inaction that gets confused with Destiny.

Observations

I don't know that any two people are fated to meet, but I think in some cases Fate stands ready to intervene if they don't.

~~~

Sometimes it's Destiny, and sometimes it's just two people who sought the same quiet corner in the same noisy room.

~~~

When it comes to bringing two people together, Fate gets a lot of credit that ought to go to Mischief.

<><><>

The Voice of Experience

I believe that Fate can bring two people together but not necessarily for the purpose of making anything easier.

~~~

I don't know if two people can share a common destiny, but I know they can share the same last chance.

~~~

'Tis a bold ballet
And a daring dance,
Dodging your destiny
And chasing your chance.

A Sad Story

"They never met, for she waited each day at the corner of Destiny and Romance, and he hung out at the corner of Main and Elm."

<><><>

Excellence

Keynote Thought

There is no bridge to excellence. It is a tightrope you walk over a sheer and sudden drop into the ordinary.

Observations

Don't expect a young person to strive for excellence who has been taught at every turn to strive for recognition and reward.

~~~

It is easier to be good at something than to be good at faking it.

~~~

You only get one life, so perhaps it is worth the effort to make it your signature life.

~~~

It is wiser to trust in the pride of workmanship than in the diligence of quality assurance.

<><><>

<>< ><>

Faith

If you would spread your faith, you must exude your faith. It is not enough that people hear it from you; they must catch it from you.

Observations

Some, tired of wondering, turn to faith for answers. Others, tired of answers, turn to faith for wonder.

~~~

Things happen in life that make us question our faith when perhaps they ought to make us question our life.

~~~

In the end it's all about faith, for without faith, there would be no hope, and without hope, there would be no motive for charity.

~~~

Of what use to appeal to reason if you lack the faith to accept its answer?

<>< ><>

<><><>

Faith

Speaking For Myself

I believe in faith and hope, although as the years go by, I find myself putting less faith in hope and more hope in faith.

~~~

I look at it this way -- if my prayers were always answered, I'd be praying to someone no wiser than I am.

~~~

I believe this -- that to be damned, you must travel the whole wayward journey. To be saved, you have only to start back.

~~~

If you will keep your eyes open to it, there is always some gosh darn thing that will restore your faith.

~~~

If you give it a central place in your life, what does it matter if you call it faith or you call it doubt?

<><><>

<>‹›<>

Family

<u>Keynote Thought</u>

In the courtroom of one's family, there is no presumption of innocence but always a mitigating circumstance.

<u>Observations</u>

To trace your family tree is to find yourself in a maze from which there is no path of escape.

~~~

You can complain of your family taking you for granted, or you can make it your achievement and your happiness.

~~~

One of the harder transitions in family life is learning to knock on a door to which for so long you held the key.

<>‹›<>

<><><>

Family

No one lacks a hope and a prayer who has a dad still hoping and a mom still praying.

~~~

Understand that the people who care about you are not trying to discourage you; they are trying to protect you from disappointment. You must appreciate them, and, of course, ignore them.

~~~

It takes a while, but eventually you realize that your mom and dad were not hypocrites but just two fallible human beings who wanted you to be better than they were.

~~~

It is a kindness to include in your life the parents of the person you were as a kid.

~~~

Nothing is so likely to make you a good and decent person as belonging to a family that operates under that assumption.

<><><>

The Family Album

What we see in an old family photo is not just a still moment in time but a moment when there was still time.

Dry, Sly and Wry

A family is a group of people that always includes someone you forgot is graduating this year.

~~~

The trouble with crediting success to skill and hard work is that it doesn't account for a successful brother-in-law.

~~~

A domestic quarrel is never about something you did. It is about something you always do.

<>‹›‹>

Forgiveness

<u>Keynote Thought</u>

*So often when you make the effort to understand,
you find that forgiveness is not required.*

<u>Observations</u>

*Some forgive and forget. Others forgive and
remember. Most forgive and remind.*

~~~

*It can be easier to forgive when you remember
that you aren't the governor, and you aren't
actually commuting anyone's sentence.*

~~~

*They are different capacities -- the willingness to
forgive others and the willingness to forgive
ourselves -- and rarely found in the same person.*

<>‹›‹>

<><><>

Friendship

Keynote Thought

A friend is not someone who badgers you to become a better person. A friend is someone who prefers you to better people.

Observations

You know you have a friend when your aimless wanderings always take you down the same street to the same address.

~~~

A best friend is someone who can detect the cry for help in the words, "I'm okay."

~~~

One of the challenges of our time is remembering which subject you must never bring up in the company of which friend.

<><><>

Friendship

Eventually you realize that not all opposing viewpoints come from people who oppose you.

~~~

Often the people in our lives who don't need an invitation need to be reminded that they don't.

Dry, Sly and Wry

One thing you learn about self-improvement is to never surprise your friends with it.

~~~

Occasionally it's good to reassess those of your friendships in which you are the only participating friend.

The Presumption of Innocence

A relative presumes you're innocent because you didn't mean it. A friend presumes you're innocent because you didn't do it.

<> <> <>

God

Keynote Thought

*To some, God is the final explanation that explains
everything. To others, God is the final mystery
that explains everything else.*

Observations

*The question, "Is God real or an invention of man?"
is something that probably matters more to man
than it does to God.*

~~~

*Too often the answer to the question, "What in
God's name were you thinking?" is that you
weren't thinking in God's name.*

~~~

*Perhaps the Creator knew this -- that we would
never fully reveal ourselves in prayer to someone
we were absolutely sure existed.*

<> <> <>

God

Perhaps God has talked to you, perhaps not, but it is more likely that He has talked to you than to some third party about you.

The Voice of Experience

No one who has someone to pray for remains long in doubt that there is Someone to pray to.

Dry. Sly and Wry

On the Seventh Day the Creator sat back, took off His gloves and said, "No fingerprints. They'll just have to find me in the sunsets."

~~~

Science is an exercise in reverse engineering by which scientists attempt to prove there was no original engineer.

<><><>

<>< ><>

Happiness

Keynote Thought

The key to happiness? Simple really. You don't let short-term concerns ruin your life, and you don't let long-term concerns ruin your day.

Observations

The hardest thing about finding real happiness is leaving behind something that seemed like it.

~~~

You can as easily find the one true recipe for happiness as you can find the one true recipe for shepherd's pie.

~~~

Some people will always allow themselves to be happy, while others will always be standing in line for the permit.

<>< ><>

<><><>

The Voice of Experience

One thing you notice about the happiest people is that they seem to have the littlest reason.

~~~

You have to let trivial things make you happy. You can't count on the important things.

~~~

Occasionally it's good to devote a day to letting someone who wants to make you happy have a go at it.

~~~

Happiness is an occasional glance into how simple it all can be.

~~~

We do not consciously choose to be unhappy. Rather we choose security over risk, stability over change, what seems permanent over what seems fleeting. We choose unhappiness because it has the better chance of lasting.

<><><>

<>‹›‹›

It is a sad thing to say about happiness that you were too busy pursuing it to have any time for it.

Speaking For Myself

Like many, I never achieved the happiness I dreamed of, having exchanged it along the way for a happiness I never dreamed of.

If You Want My Advice

Do what makes you happy, and trust in the wisdom of your happiness.

The Search For Happiness

How little you know,
As you follow its track,
How much of the search
Will be circling back.

Hope

Keynote Thought

There is a state of denial called hope which is usually more productive than the state of denial called despair.

Observations

You find hope the same way you find happiness -- you give it to someone else and borrow a little of it back.

~~~

Advice once heard: "Head always in the direction of your hopes and dreams -- and don't listen to anyone who passes you, headed back."

~~~

Hope is not a plan, but, without it, nothing else is a plan, either.

<><><>

Hope

The difference between hope and wishful thinking is that you can build on hope whereas wishful thinking is always a strategy in itself.

The Voice of Experience

Life is a gradual transformation from having faith in hope to having hope in faith.

~~~

Never lose hope, because miracles happen and they need something to work with.

<><><>

Humankind

Keynote Thought

Some day a computer will give a wrong answer to spare someone's feelings, and man will have invented artificial intelligence.

Observations

Nothing is so underrated as the independent streak it takes to be a normal everyday person.

~~~

You discover this -- that when you leave behind your preconceived notions of people, you rarely go back for them.

~~~

Is is true of most human beings that if they had no physical body, they would still have an identifying scar.

<><><>

*Which of us is not a wanderer in this world,
convinced that everyone else knows where they're
going.*

~~~

*It takes no skill to scoff at the pretenses of others,
to strip people of their transparent masks. It takes
only a larger pretense, a more subtle mask.*

~~~

*We are, each of us, a private soul hiding behind a
public mask, complaining that our private soul
gets no understanding.*

~~~

*Nobody's perfect, and our fondest memories of
anyone are of the hilarious ways they proved it.*

Overheard in a Pet Shop

*"I have nothing against the human race. I just
think there are better role models for our kids."*

<><><>

The Voice of Experience

The surest way to learn something about human nature is to try to teach it something.

~~~

Nothing is so under-appreciated as the collateral good done by simple people seeking their own honest ends.

~~~

It is possible to find something good in everyone. The trick is to stop right there.

Dry. Sly and Wry

In the end you must accept the human race as a fact, however much you might have rejected it as a proposal.

~~~

In a day and age when so much is believed without supporting evidence, why not believe there's a little good in everyone?

<><><>

Speaking For Myself

I don't know what it takes to be you, and you don't know what it takes to be me, and so we tend to underrate each other's courage.

~~~

We can be all in this together or all in this apart, but make no mistake, we are all in this.

~~~

I've learned this -- that it's impossible to understand another human being using just what you know about them.

~~~

I guess if I had it all to do over, I'd give everything a little more time and everyone a little more space.

~~~

I wouldn't say that all human beings are 100% the same -- maybe 96% the same with a 4% margin of error.

<><><>

<>&<>&<>

Ignorance

Keynote Thought

Just as darkness is the absence of light, ignorance is the absence of knowledge -- and should not be mistaken for an alternative point of view.

Observations

One of life's mysteries is how anyone can become more ignorant.

~~~

You underrate ignorance if you think if can be fooled by new evidence.

~~~

The trouble with people who never learn is that they never seem to be finished doing it.

~~~

To the ignorant, it is not called learning; it is called flip-flopping.

<>&<>&<>

<></><>

The Journey

Keynote Thought

I remember well the road I took and the friends I traveled with. Did we ever get to where we were going? That I don't recall.

Observations

The surest sign that you're on the right path is that you like the company you're keeping.

~~~

No one who has wandered the world alone has ever confused it with traveling.

~~~

There's the hard way and the easy way. The thing about the hard way is that you don't usually waste your life looking for it.

<></><>

<><>

Judgment

Keynote Thought

I have learned to give people the benefit of the doubt, because, to be honest, I don't know a lot of people who have benefited from my certainty.

Observations

If you refrain from judging people until you really know them, you often don't have to judge them at all.

<center>~~~</center>

Nobody's perfect, in case you thought you were perfect -- or in case you thought you were nobody.

If You Want My Advice

Stay out of the court of self-judgment, for the jury has already formed an opinion.

<><>

Judgment

Never confuse having all the facts with knowing the whole story.

~~~

Be reluctant to judge, for it is hard to know another person's true intent -- or the true intent of the judge.

Dry, Sly and Wry

Always, before assigning blame, consider the possibility that it might be that bleeping butterfly, flapping its wings in Mongolia.

<><><>

<><><>

Leadership

Keynote Thought

Leadership is the gentle art of planting a thought is someone's head just before it occurs to them.

Observations

There is no more important leadership skill than the ability to interpret blank looks as "the ayes have it."

~~~

Anyone who knows what they want from life becomes a irresistible magnet to everyone who doesn't.

~~~

The first job of a team leader is to identify the two or three people who will do all the work and keep everyone else out of their way.

<><><>

<><><>

Learning

Keynote Thought

You spend years learning what's important and one heart-stopping moment learning what's more important.

Observations

The best proof that you are still capable of learning is that there's something you recently unlearned.

~~~

One thing that varies from person to person is how many times you have to do a fool thing before you learn not to do it twice.

~~~

Experience is a patient teacher, always willing to repeat the lesson for slow learners.

~~~

Kids learn by their mistakes, and one of the harder things we do as parents or teachers is not to stand in the way of the process.

<><><>

<>< ><>

Life

Keynote Thought

Perhaps, because life is but a moment, it is insignificant, or, perhaps, because life is but a moment, it is momentous.

Observations

At some point you just have to let heredity and environment debate themselves while you go off and shape your own life.

~~~

It is said that you only get one life. In truth, you only get one birth and one death. How many lives you squeeze in is up to you.

~~~

There are tragedies in life that change us forever, the person we once were mistakenly listed among the survivors.

<>< ><>

Life gives us the minutes and the hours. We create the moments and the occasions.

Advice From An Older Head

Occasionally it's good to pause, take a moment and inventory the things in your life that are just fine.

~~~

It is a missed opportunity not to idle away the few precious moments of life intended for that purpose.

~~~

It is a sad thing, at the end of your life, to look in a mirror and see the only person you forgot to please.

~~~

Whatever else you think about life, it's the best test ever designed to find out who your friends are.

<>< ><>

<><><>

Life

An easy life is never so fondly recalled as the happy moments in a hard one.

<center>~~~</center>

It is generally a more productive day when you learn something from life rather than try to teach it something.

<u>Life is...</u>

Life is an educational process you can't opt out of. You either learn the lesson, or you become the lesson.

<center>~~~</center>

Life is a brief moment in eternity when you can't claim you were somewhere else at the time.

<center>~~~</center>

Life is a series of paths you don't know you're choosing... decisions you don't know you're making... farewells you don't know you're saying.

<><><>

<>< ><>

Listening

Keynote Thought

Learn to hold your tongue, and you will be fluent in every language and on all topics.

Observations

The first thing to learn about the art of conversation is that you are not the other person's favorite subject.

~~~

You don't have to have an opinion about everything, and if you do, not everyone has to know what it is.

~~~

One way to meet new people is to listen a little more carefully to the people you see every day.

<>< ><>

<><><>

Listening

Sometimes the wisest thing to do is just sit back quietly and let people come to their senses.

Speaking For Myself

I have learned to just quietly listen, finding that it is usually what people want when they ask for my input.

Dry, Sly and Wry

The advantage of silence over words is that there's a wider range of things you can claim you didn't mean by it.

~~~

Just standing there with a blank look on your face is better than uttering words to that effect.

<><><>

<>< ><>

Loneliness

Keynote Thought

*It is possible to live a simple, uncomplicated life, but
we usually call it by another name. We call it
loneliness.*

Observations

*Two's company, three's a crowd, which leaves us to
discover for ourselves what one is.*

~~~

*It is often true of two lonely people that if they would
turn and retrace their steps, they would meet.*

~~~

*One sign of loneliness is when a stranger gives you
the time of day, and you wonder if it might deepen
into love.*

~~~

*Loneliness is not a physical thing. Not everyone who
lives alone is lonely, and not every street person is
living on the street.*

<>< ><>

<>‹>‹>

Loss of a Child

(Written after the Oklahoma City bombing on April 19, 1995.)

A Mother's Reverie

Child lost, do you suppose
That we could ever be apart,
That though you've left my yearning bosom,
You could ever leave my heart?

Do you suppose that though the years
Bring what they will of joy and strife,
I'll e'er forget that once there stirred
Within me your sweet precious life?

Do you suppose that there will come
A morning when I'll not arise
To live again that day when last
You turned to me your trusting eyes?

Child dear, I know you dwell
Within the Lord's protective might,
But do you know how brave you were
And how I long to hold you tight?

<>‹>‹>

<> <> <>

Love

Keynote Thought

It is such a simple sentiment, "I love you" and yet so hard sometimes to get the words right.

Observations

The promise to love forever is always based on the merest taste of love and the tiniest sampling of forever.

~~~

There is no more exciting opportunity in life than to meet a beautiful person who has never been sufficiently informed of the fact.

~~~

Love can be a conversation about nothing, or it can be a quiet comfort in each other's presence that is about everything.

<> <> <>

<><><>

Love

You can live in an unfair world, feeling that somehow you deserve it -- until one day you meet someone who clearly doesn't.

~~~

The proof that you are loved is not that your perfections are praised but that your imperfections are defended.

~~~

Only in love can you get blindsided by something you saw coming.

~~~

The illusion that love weaves is not just that your partner is perfect but that you are perfectible.

~~~

How do you find love? You just keep showing a brave face to the world, and one day it melts someone's heart.

<><><>

<></><>

In the end, you don't need to know what love is. You just need to know that certain people are safe from harm.

The Voice of Experience

For every person who thinks they can never be loved, there is another person, somewhere, who thinks they can never love.

~~~

Yes, there are reasons no one could love you, and you can be sure your lover knows them all.

~~~

No one ever falls in love for the purpose of debating the wisdom of the move.

~~~

Can you love someone too much? Perhaps, but that is not usually the question that haunts your memories when they are gone.

<></><>

<>＜>＜>

Marriage

Keynote Thought

It's nice to know the definition of love, but it's probably more important to know the definition of partner.

Observations

Perhaps the marriage vows could use a promise of a little conversation at dinner and an occasional stroll together at sunset.

~~~

How to make a marriage last? You work at it every day, and once a year you celebrate the anniversary of the same wedding.

~~~

It's a rare marriage where you don't sometimes wish you could go back and marry an impartial third party.

<>＜><>

<><><>

Not every good friendship is a marriage, but every good marriage is a friendship.

~~~

It helps when the vows you exchange at the altar are something you already shook hands on.

~~~

The hardest thing in marriage is to trust after having been certain.

Dry, Sly and Wry

Marriage -- one of the longer-term commitments we make in our quest for instant gratification.

~~~

There are ways to express love so subtle that they are undetectable by a third party -- or in a long marriage, by the second party.

~~~

To be many-years married is to have a partner who can finish your sentences -- although not usually the way you would.

<><><>

<><><>

Memories

Keynote Thought

*I enjoy, occasionally, a day with my memories --
those paintings hanging on the walls of my mind.*

Observations

*Ah, nostalgia. We live our days in the glare of the
sun and recall them in the glow of the moon.*

~~~

*How different might be our memories if the person
who lived them had ever imagined the person who
would recall them.*

~~~

*It is hard to say which is more indelible in memory --
the anxious minute that lasted forever or the
comfortable forever that lasted a minute.*

<><><>

<><><>

Miracles

Keynote Thought

One of the things we are allowed to decide for ourselves is whether we wish to have miracles in our lives.

Observations

We pray for divine intervention, and then one day it hits us -- that we are the tool by which God intervenes, that our prayer was answered on the day we were born.

~~~

We don't always get the miracle we pray for, but we always get the strength we pray for.

~~~

You can wait for a miracle, but it's usually a better strategy to meet it halfway,

<><><>

<><><>

Miracles

Not everyone believes in miracles or prayer, but everyone, at some point, prays for a miracle.

~~~

The difference between a miracle and luck is that you can have luck without believing in it.

<u>*Overheard*</u>

"Do I believe in miracles? I believe in God. It is the atheist who must believe in miracles."

<><><>

<><><>

Mom

Keynote Thought

Those times you did not see her tears,
Do you think she didn't cry?
Those times you could not bear the truth.
Do you think she didn't lie?
Those times you wished she loved you less,
Do you think she didn't try?

Observations

Mom -- the person most likely to write an
autobiography and never mention herself.

~ ~ ~

The unique thing about a mother's love is that the
less of it you deserve, the more of it you get.

~ ~ ~

Ever wonder why someone would give up the
leading role in her own life story to play the mom in
yours?

<><><>

<><><>

Morality

The time to wonder if you're doing the right thing is when it seems to be getting easier.

Observations

Evil never asks for commitment. It is the free trial you lose track of that automatically renews at full price.

~~~

Good always has opportunity. We need to give it motive. Evil always has motive. We need to deny it opportunity.

~~~

The list keeps growing -- the evils condoned by otherwise good people -- until there is no otherwise left.

<><><>

<>

Pure evil does not represent itself as evil but as purity.

~~~

Nothing supports evil like the assumption of good people that there is a line it will not cross.

~~~

What good is a moral code that causes you to regret but never causes you to reconsider?

~~~

If good can learn something from evil, it is to have greater faith in what one person can do.

The Voice of Experience

It's never fun, but sometimes there's a battle you have to lose to know you're on the right side.

~~~

If it makes you feel more like a fool than a saint, it's probably the right thing to do.

<>

<>< ><>

Morality

How do you become a good person? You practice the mannerisms until they become your own.

~~~

A good time to pause and reexamine your life is when you find yourself supporting the devil because he shares your values.

Speaking For Myself

If I try to do the right thing, it is not so that people will say, "Thank you," but so that people will say, "I thought it was you."

~~~

There are things you've done that come back to haunt you -- and things that haunt you that you're still doing.

A Question

Is there a religion that would not benefit from calling home its missionaries and setting them to work among its hypocrites?

<>< ><>

<>‹›‹›

Opportunity

<u>Keynote Thought</u>

You can plan a picnic, hoping for a sunny day, but sometimes a sunny day just pops up and requires your immediate attention.

<u>Observations</u>

The problem, in a busy life, is that opportunity always knocks at an inopportune moment -- and rarely leaves a message.

~~~

We never forget our lost opportunities. It is our excuses we would have had to make a note of.

~~~

The most important lesson we learn in life is how to recognize our last chance.

<>‹›‹›

<><><>

Optimism

*One morning, in a spring that seemed
forever dark and drear,
the sun was on the meadow,
and a fragrance filled the air,
and those who had succumbed to thoughts
of sadness and despair
were caught again, as usual,
completely unaware.*

Observations

*Optimism is the knack of not letting every single
thing that could ruin your life ruin your day.*

~~~

*You don't have to be an optimist to know that many a
bright day hides in a morning mist.*

~~~

*The optimist believes in a just God, not because it is
the only conceivable faith but because it is the only
conceivable reason for optimism.*

<><><>

<>< ><>

Parentlng

All you can do as a parent is to make the recommended mistakes at the recommended age and trust to God.

Observations

One of the harder things we do as parents is to allow our kids their disappointments.

~~~

What you don't appreciate as a kid is that if your parents are always going to be there for you, they aren't going to be somewhere else, doing exciting and glamorous things.

~~~

To be a parent is to feel that when something bad happens to you and you alone, it has taken the decoy.

<>< ><>

<><><>

The Voice of Experience

Our kids do not follow our preachings; they follow us.

~~~

Nothing we do for our kids quite repays what they do for us, which is to present us the world brand-new again.

Dry, Sly and Wry

Parenting (as described by a parent): a calling where nothing you do right makes any difference and everything you do wrong has lifelong consequences.

~~~

What's missing from most "How To" books on parenting is how to be on the receiving end of it.

~~~

Adolescence never changes. What changes are the generations of parents wondering what they did wrong.

<><><>

<><><>

Passage

Keynote Thought

One thing to remember in setting the priorities in your life is that your employer does not usually write your obituary.

Observations

The thing about people who understand you is that when they die, you can still visit them, and they still understand you.

~~~

You don't have to believe in an afterlife to believe that there are people gone from this earth you can still make proud of you.

~~~

One thing you sadly notice over the years is how often the words, "This doesn't mean goodbye" mean goodbye.

<><><>

<><><>

Perception

Keynote Thought

Once you perceive yourself as a victim of circumstances, the supply of circumstances becomes infinite.

Observations

Nothing lasts forever, but it's hard to think of a human emotion that doesn't assume something will.

~~~

In a world of self-confident bluster, do not undervalue the charm of seeming quiet and unassuming and, at times, a little lost.

~~~

A perception we nearly always have wrong is that someone in our lives would be better off without us.

~~~

One thing certain about anyone you think has had an easy life is that they are not personally aware of it.

<><><>

<><><>

Perseverance

Keynote Thought

You can charge ahead and trust to fortune, or you can take small daily steps and trust to inevitability.

Observations

You can lose the battle and win the war. You can even lose the war and win the post war.

~~~

A partial action is better than a full intention.

~~~

There is no actual law that says that when things go wrong, you can't pick up your own pieces.

What Shall I Be?

What shall I be -- the angry sea
That pounds against the shore
Or soft agleam, the quiet stream.
That carves the canyon floor?

<><><>

<><><>

Pets

Keynote Thought

A pet is so often the answer -- when you're lonely and need company, or when you're tired of company and need lonely.

Observations

It is challenge enough for any day to live up to your dog's opinion of you -- and maybe pleasantly surprise your cat.

~~~

Ever wonder if there's the same sad look in your dog's eyes when he or she is looking at someone else?

~~~

Perhaps the reason why pets hold such a special place in our hearts is that they appreciate so much any place at all.

<><><>

Speaking For Myself

When I think of the loyalty of pets, I think of Adam and Eve leaving paradise, followed by their dog.

~~~

What makes our pets' forgiveness so remarkable is that you can be darn sure they haven't forgotten.

Dry, Sly and Wry

It is rare that pets conspire against their owners. When seen huddled together, they are more likely planning an intervention.

~~~

A dog is man's best friend. A cat is man's best formal acquaintance.

~~~

A pet -- this creature who never judges us, or, rather, whose always reliable forgiveness gives that impression.

<> <> <>

Politics

<u>Keynote Thought</u>

Time -- that which heals all sorrows, reveals all lies and rights all wrongs. In other words, retires all politicians.

<u>Observations</u>

Politics is a game of chess, and what we know about a game of chess is that the pawns will be sacrificed.

~~~

Once there were kings and queens, and we were all subjects. Now there are politicians, and we are all objects.

~~~

To condone a political injustice is simply to take your place in the line of eventual victims.

<>< ><>

You know something's wrong with a political system when you have to beg for justice as if it were mercy.

~~~

A political party is like any other conspiracy. The people it conspires against suppose they are part of it.

The Voice of Experience

Never, in politics, suppose that you have heard the whole truth. Indeed, never suppose that you have heard the whole lie.

Dry, Sly and Wry

As between God, country and apple pie, politicians have done the least damage in the name of apple pie.

~~~

You just hope that a politician who claims to know what you deserve is better informed on other subjects.

<><><>

<><><>

Possessions

Keynote Thought

Be careful of what you become in order to get things, because one day the things you got will be gone, and you will be left with only what you've become.

Observations

Of what use to have a houseful of things if none of them greets you as you walk through the front door?

~~~

The most foolish thing we do in our quest for more is to risk what is already enough.

~~~

It is hard to be happy with what you have if you dwell always on what you deserve.

<><><>

Material wealth is always tempered by the recollection that there was some sort of happiness that was supposed to come with it.

~~~

It is not the wealthy who shape the world but they who have no price.

~~~

Possession is nine-tenths of the law. One suspects it is a smaller part of happiness.

Speaking For Myself

There are things I have wanted so long that I would only consent to have them if I could keep wanting them.

<> <> <>

Possibility

Keynote Thought

*As important as keeping a grasp on reality is
keeping a grasp on possibility.*

Observations

*Not everything unknown to science is unknown to
possibility.*

~~~

*What no one thought possible, one enterprising
individual accomplishes, and then everyone has an
idea how to do it better.*

~~~

*Understand that the odds against you have nothing
to do with you. They are merely the odds against
the average person who has attempted to do it up to
now.*

<> <> <>

<>< ><>

Reality

Keynote Thought

What is reality but the dreamworld of a limited imagination.

Observations

By all means, accept reality -- but be sure to subscribe to the monthly updates.

~~~

Never give up an illusion until you have exhausted all its possibilities.

~~~

So often when people tell you you must accept reality, it is not the reality they accepted.

~~~

There is a point in life when the quest becomes the reality and going home again the impossible dream.

<>< ><>

<><><>

Reality

You might say this about reality -- that nothing in human history has proved itself so willing to compromise in order to be accepted.

~~~

It is always when things are bleakest that we are told we must accept reality, as if you could not accept reality on a bright, sunny day.

Speaking For Myself

If I do not always accept reality, it is because I have looked behind the curtain and seen how it's done.

~~~

I reject the notion that just because you call it reality, it doesn't have to meet some minimum standard.

~~~

I look at it this way -- reality is the furniture. I'm the interior decorator.

<><><>

<><><>

Reconciliation

Keynote Thought

The most important next step is the one you take to meet someone half way.

Observations

The best solution seldom requires that someone be right and someone else be wrong.

~~~

So often the path to reconciliation is the length of an about face.

~~~

You can call it betrayal, or you can recognize that true love makes impossible promises.

~~~

Anger, frustration, resentment -- there are a hundred different names for a little time that needs to go by.

<><><>

<>＜><>

Regret

<u>Keynote Thought</u>

*If only regret had action's purpose. If only action
had regret's information.*

<u>Observations</u>

*For every person who atones, a hundred find regret
sufficient.*

~~~

*Essential to happiness is the ability to discard one's
regrets once they have served their purpose.*

~~~

*We act today with our excuses and regret tomorrow
with our real reasons.*

~~~

*The most common cause of acting too late is
regretting too early,*

<>＜><>

Speaking For Myself

*I refuse to regret based on what I know now,
having so much to regret based on what I knew at
the time.*

~~~

*"I regret it, but there's nothing I can do about it" I
tell myself, wondering if I would regret it
otherwise.*

The Voice of Experience

*One way to stop doing things you later regret is to
stop doing things you already regret.*

~~~

*Sometimes there are words said and regretted that
need to be said -- and regretted.*

~~~

*So often you head off a decision you'll later regret
by looking into your heart and finding regret
already there.*

<><><>

Relationships

Keynote Thought

There are times in a relationship when the band plays, but mostly you dance to a remembered tune.

Observations

There are days when two people who have committed to each other light years beyond friendship need to just be friends.

~~~

Whether a relationship begins by fate or chance, it nearly always endures by second chance.

~~~

It is sad to complicate a simple thing, but it is sadder to lose a simple thing because you were unwilling to complicate it.

<>< ><>

So often in a relationship you fail to put two-and-two together because you want so much to keep one-and-one together.

~~~

There is no bond so instantly recognized in a glance across a barroom as a common desire to go down in flames.

The Voice of Experience

It's amazing the relationship you can build on just being two people willing to take a chance.

~~~

It is rare in a relationship that we need to hear words that our partner doesn't need to hear also.

~~~

A general rule in relationships is that if it used to matter, it still does.

~~~

There is a tendency in a relationship to become whomever you must become in order to avoid further discussion of the topic.

<><><>

Responsibility

Keynote Thought

Life -- a brief moment in eternity when you can't claim you were somewhere else at the time.

Observations

A salute today to every blameless person who ever took the blame in order to just get on with it.

~~~

If it's justice you want, blame those responsible. If it's action you want, blame yourself.

~~~

Actions have consequences, often mistaken for a run of bad luck.

~~~

I didn't know because I didn't ask. I didn't hear because I didn't listen. I didn't see because I looked away. So, you see, I was not to blame.

Retirement

Keynote Thought

You can look at it as another ho-hum day in retirement, or you can look at it as another day of successfully avoiding the paparazzi.

Observations

The secret to doing fun things in retirement is to have a spouse who has already bought the tickets and already made the reservations.

~~~

I don't call it sleeping in my chair. I call it devoting an afternoon to activities that don't require my personal supervision.

~~~

You watch a lot of TV in retirement -- some programs because you enjoy them, others because the remote is six inches beyond your reach.

<><><>

Self-Awareness

Keynote Thought

What we never see in a mirror is the smile that greets our friends or the blush that welcomes our lover.

Observations

It all comes down to self-esteem. To be capable of compassion and tolerance, indeed to be capable of humility, you must be able look in a mirror and like the person you see.

~~~

It takes a while, but eventually you realize that limiting your horizons to your own selfish interests limits your horizons.

~~~

While I sometimes wonder what people might think of me, I mostly wonder what might make them start.

We each have two reputations -- the one by which we are known to the world and the one by which we are known to ourselves. There is still time to repair the second.

Speaking For Myself

I have come to believe this about self-esteem -- that a unwarranted sense of it is better than none.

Dry, Sly and Wry

It is hard to look in a mirror and believe that you are someone's great love. On the other hand, it does seem likelier than infatuation.

~~~

<>‹›‹›

Soul Mates

Keynote Thought

There is a moment in life when you discover that it's not all about you -- usually when you meet the person it's all about.

Observations

To find a loving partner is never again to doubt those moments in Scripture when an angel appears.

~~~

It's not about finding fun things to do. It's about finding someone in whose company, it's all fun.

~~~

Sweeter than any success is having someone you can't wait to tell about it.

~~~

It isn't the end of the world as long as there is someone in your world to tell you it isn't.

<>‹›‹›

<>< ><>

*It is rare that two people can remember what they
were looking for when they found each other.*

Novels in One Line

*"She was a stroller in the sand, a walker in the rain,
a frequenter of places where nobody goes--and they
kept meeting."*

~~~

*"It was a rainy night when, chasing her destiny, she
wandered into his last chance."*

~~~

<>< ><>

Success

Keynote Thought

The trick to succeeding is to stop thinking there's a trick to everything.

Observations

What you notice about successful people is that they don't always look as fresh at the end of the day as they did at the beginning.

~~~

You can write a success story, or a hard-luck story, out of the same set of excuses.

~~~

If at first you don't succeed, you at least find out who your friends are.

~~~

So often the idea that something's stopping you is an obstacle illusion.

<><><>

*The way to duplicate another's success is to
duplicate their journey.*

~~~

*I could tell you the secret to success if I knew what
part of getting up, dressed and out the door were a
secret.*

~~~

*So often the people we forget to thank for our
success are the people who never offered us less.*

The Voice of Experience

*It is for those who would happily settle for second
place that there are third-place prizes.*

~~~

*To achieve success, you must not only ignore your
critics, you must ignore friends telling you you did
the best you could.*

~~~

*Never taking a chance is a way to lose without ever
having a chance to win.*

<><><>

<>&<>&<>

Time

Keynote Thought

The past is but mem'ries,
The future but dreams.
Only the present
Is just what it seems.

Observations

Life is short, except for the endless hours, and long,
except for the fleeting years.

~~~

Time is the one resource in life that when it's all
spent, you wish you had spent more of it foolishly.

~~~

If there is a first rule in the management of time, it
is to always keep a spare moment in your hip
pocket.

<>&<>&<>

You cannot return to a time, but sometimes, together, you can return to a beginning.

~~~

It is a lesser regret to have spent time foolishly than to have let it expire unused.

~~~

People who would never trespass on your property will trespass on your time, as if your time were not your property.

~~~

The present oft replays the past,
Same old drama, different cast,
The former cast, you somehow sense,
Sitting in the audience.

The Voice of Experience

Time - that which reveals all lies, revises all forecasts and renders inadequate all excuses.

<><><>

<><><>

Tolerance

Keynote Thought

It is no secret but worth repeating. At the core of all prejudice is self-loathing. At the heart of all tolerance is self-respect.

Observations

An important corollary to the Golden Rule is to leave others be as you would have them leave you be.

~~~

The thing to realize about your prejudices is that they love to pose as your principles.

~~~

If all sins were forgivable, we wouldn't need forgiveness. If all people deserved mercy, we wouldn't need mercy.

<><><>

<>‹>‹>

The Voice of Experience

A good part of tolerance is just letting others live by the same deceptions we allow ourselves.

~~~

There is a tendency to treat unjustly those whose only crime is that we have treated them unjustly.

~~~

Which of us has ever cast our eye from our neighbor's child to our own without changing lens?

Speaking For Myself

I have never considered it my business to rid someone of a belief that makes life tolerable for them.

~~~

I wonder, often, how cruelty became so tolerable and the simple aspirations of the human soul so threatening.

<>‹>‹>

<><><>

Trust

Keynote Thought

*One thing you never know is whether the person who
fell into the trap your suspicion set would have
flourished in the arms of your trust.*

Observations

*It is unlikely that a child taught to distrust others will
make an exception of the teacher.*

~~~

*It is hard in a relationship when certainty is reduced
to trust, and harder still when trust is reduced to
hope.*

~~~

*What you often find in a trusting relationship is a
trap never sprung because it was never set.*

<><><>

<><><>

Truth and Lies

<u>Keynote Thought</u>

The truth is more often a lone voice than a chorus, especially when the chorus is in perfect harmony.

<u>Observations</u>

It is tolerable -- the lie that gets you through your days, if you can return to a truth that gets you through your nights.

~~~

The attraction of a lie is that it invites us into an exclusive club, whereas the truth welcomes all.

~~~

What a clever liar eventually learns is that telling the truth would have been more clever.

~~~

Too often a devotion to the truth is confused with knowing what the truth is.

<><><>

<><><>

Truth and Lies

The Voice of Experience

It is a sad regret to have searched for the truth and settled for an answer.

~~~

It is a common misconception that people who lie and cheat to get what they want know what they want.

~~~

The hardest thing about discovering a lie is not that it shakes your trust but that it changes your memories.

Speaking For Myself

Perhaps I can't handle the truth, but it is a short list of people I would trust to make that judgment for me.

~~~

Always be prepared to do what you plan to do when people find out the truth.

<><><>

<>< ><>

Wisdom

Keynote Thought

Wisdom is not what you know but how quickly you adjust when the opposite proves true.

Observations

Wisdom is mostly knowing when to change the subject.

~~~

To be ultimately wise is to know everything, none of it for sure.

~~~

A good part of wisdom is being lost for words when the situation calls for it.

~~~

The wise do not ponder the meaning of life. Life is getting the kids off to school and the dog fed. It is the meaning of meaning they ponder.

<>< ><>

Wisdom

If You Want My Advice

If you can't be wise, be happy, and trust in the wisdom of your happiness.

Dry, Sly and Wry

The aphorist sees in every truth a wise saying -- and in every contradiction, two wise sayings.

~~~

It is not wisdom until you learn it too late.

<><><>

Women

Keynote Thought

Only a man is allowed to give up. There is always someone for whom a woman must carry on.

Observations

What a woman wants from a man is love. What a man wants from a woman is hope.

~~~

If the human race ever becomes civilized, it will be the story of how a species called man became woman.

~~~

A toast today to all the jobs that magically do themselves -- and to the women who do them.

~~~

I had a dream where I asked God, "Are you real or did man invent you?" And God said, "Actually, it was a woman."

<><><>

<><><>

Writing

Keynote Thought

If it doesn't work horizontally as prose,
it
probably
won't
work
any
better
vertically
pretending
to be
poetry.

You Are Probably a Writer

Look about you. Is there some physical tool --
brush, chisel, musical instrument -- whose use you
have mastered? Is there a part of your body --
voice, hands, feet -- that responds utterly to your
command? If so, you are an artist. If not, you are
probably a writer.

<><><>

<u>Uncategorized</u>

A few thoughts where my thinking cap failed to produce enough lines to flesh out a full-page topic.

~~~

<><><>

<><><>

Uncategorized

What I remember most fondly about childhood is that there were explanations for things, and they were fascinating.

~~~

Only in the play world of a child's imagination is there a reason for everything.

~~~

In the life we might have lived, the years never pass. On the person we might have been, age never leaves its mark. How different would seem our might-have-beens if we could see them as they would be now.

~~~

Count no day lost in which you let be that which needed to be let be.

~~~

Sadly, there's a tendency to let the same thing keep making you unhappy while requiring that happiness be always something new and different.

<><><>

<>‹›‹›

Is it worth it -- spending your life climbing the social ladder in order to hobnob with people who got there by helicopter?

~~~

It is when there aren't any words to say that it's so important to show up and leave them thoughtfully unsaid.

~~~

The problem with leaving behind a wasted planet is figuring out how to leave it behind.

~~~

Always keep your home presentable, assuming you keep a home for purposes of presentation.

~~~

Once there was a couple who parted to go their separate ways only to discover that they didn't have any ways that were separate.

~~~

I have always enjoyed expressing myself in music. My instrument? My two hands applauding the band.

<>‹›‹›

<><><>

Uncategorized

Most of what we know of the human soul goes by the name of music appreciation.

~~~

You don't take over a room by making people feel small. You take over a room by making people feel noticed.

~~~

Never be more insistent until you have tried being less insistent.

~~~

The lesson of history is that most advances are by half-step, most progress by partial success.

~~~

When you are going around in circles, it is not progress to report an increase in circles completed.

~~~

Each morning I gaze at the eastern horizon, and if the sun keeps its promise, I keep mine.

~~~

You can wander a loneliness alone, but a solitude wants to be shared.

<><><>

<><><>

<u>Afterthoughts</u>

A wry and whimsical set, a bit curmudgeonly at times. Here and there, I have allowed our resident cynic a brief, whiny voice. Do read on, but expect more in the way of amusement than uplift.

~~~

<><><>

Afterthoughts

*Before you criticize a boastful person, remember --
it's hard to be humble when no one is proud of you.*

~~~

*Why worry? It isn't the end of the world. And if it
is, why worry?*

~~~

*There is a reason for everything, if you don't always
insist that it be adequate.*

~~~

*You learn by doing, and what you principally learn
is not to do it again.*

~~~

*It's curious how a person can say, "She sells
seashells by the seashore" but can't say, "I love you."*

You get to a point in life where you'd settle for life, liberty and the pursuit of can't complain.

~~~

Meanwhile, the traffic control helicopter reports a three-mile backup on the road less traveled by.

~~~

You have to believe that there's a little good in everyone, although if there isn't, that would explain everything.

~~~

Never explain, until you find that one special person who understands your inner soul, and then, God help them.

~~~

It is asking a lot of friends and relatives that they be experts in the interpretation of silences.

~~~

Nothing so often turns the truth into a lie as the words, "Present company excluded."

<><><>

Afterthoughts

*I've discovered this -- that it's important to have a
friend who won't lie to you. I mean, besides a friend
who will.*

~~~

*Marriage is a state of bliss in which if you die
unexpectedly, your spouse is the prime suspect.*

~~~

*To say, "I'm going to hate myself for this," assumes
that you ever know why you hate yourself.*

~~~

*I'd rather trust in God than Lady Luck because, to be
honest, I'm not that sure Lady Luck even exists.*

~~~

*You learn this -- it's hard to tell the truth without
somebody resenting its implications.*

~~~

If flattery is a sin, it is usually a sin of omission.

<><><>

<>< ><>

Afterthoughts

One reason to learn from history is that it's such a good example of what happens when you don't.

~~~

Nobody wants free advice. If you want to give advice, you must charge by the hour and see only by appointment.

~~~

You learn this -- that if you want a younger person to take your advice, don't always be right.

~~~

Yes, I've been accused of wasting my time, to which I reply, "Whose time did you say that was again?"

~~~

One thing I know is that I'll never plead temporary insanity, there be so little proof that it's temporary.

~~~

It is a rare person that goes off to consult God and doesn't return with at least one new commandment.

<>< ><>

<><><>

Afterthoughts

*You wonder sometimes if remaining ignorant in the
Information Age is an art or a skill.*

~~~

*Every good speech contains a summary that would
have made a great speech.*

~~~

*Never trust a list of reasons that extends beyond the
first one.*

~~~

*I guess, if I had it to do over, I'd devote more time to
things that require no action on my part.*

~~~

*Of yesterday's argument, she said, "It's water over
the dam," and he said, "No, it's water under the
bridge," and so began another argument.*

~~~

*It's hard to talk sense to people who oppose it on
principle.*

<><><>

<>< ><>

The reason we blame the messenger is that the messenger always seems to be enjoying it so much.

~~~

The hardest thing about reshaping minds is getting to them before the cement dries.

~~~

The only words more motivating than "You can do it!" are the words, "You are making a big mistake."

~~~

It is always easier to find a politician who knows what you deserve than to deserve it.

~~~

Who would not travel back in time and do the right thing, unless, of course, it were possible.

~~~

They who warn of temptation rearing its ugly head have obviously not seen temptation.

<>< ><>

Afterthoughts

There's nothing like someone saying, "What do you have to lose?" to bring something immediately to mind.

~~~

Ah, yes, the real me -- someone I'm reasonably sure my parents would never have let me play with.

~~~

There are personal secrets I would not reveal under torture. I mean, there would have to be a silence at a cocktail party, or you would have to be sitting next to me in tourist class.

~~~

Over the course of a lifetime, we are many different people occupying the same body, not all familiar with the etiquette of time-sharing.

~~~

Whoever dreamed up Scrabble had an exaggerated idea of how many seven-letter words have five i's.

<><><>

Afterthoughts

One shudders to think, which is why so many have given up the practice.

~~~

God left so many fingerprints at the scene of Creation that you wonder -- does He want to be found, or does He want to be stopped?

~~~

As a gardener, I wonder if flowers really can't speak or just exercise unfailingly good judgment in the matter.

~~~

The trouble with the question, "What can possibly go wrong?" is that it rules out most of what can go wrong.

~~~

Irony? It's like when you don't believe in miracles, and you die in an accident where police say, "It's a miracle only one person died."

<><><>

Afterthoughts

It is a rare sinner who doesn't know who his forgivers will be.

~~~

Just when you think a politician knows better, you discover he knows worse.

~~~

Everyone wants to be liked, often mistaken for wanting to be understood.

~~~

No child ever learned a lesson by being spared the lesson.

~~~

If only mankind could start over again -- and this time try it as womankind.

~~~

What makes a charge of neglect seem so unfair is that usually you weren't even there.

<><><>

<><><>

The easiest way to remove the clutter from your life is to leave the clutter where it is and put yourself out on the curb.

~~~

No matter what it is, it's always better to discover it yourself than have it brought to your attention.

~~~

There are tons of man-made debris orbiting the Earth, in case you thought that man's ability to pollute the atmosphere required an atmosphere.

~~~

Before you say to me, "There is no easy way to tell you this," understand that I'm willing to wait until there is.

~~~

Did you hear? The FBI arrested a guy with a printing press who was running a stimulus program out of his basement.

<><><>

<><><>

Afterthoughts

One cure for road rage is to realize that everyone on the FBI's "Ten Most Wanted" list probably drives.

~~~

It is still possible to be a blind optimist. Also helps if you're hard of hearing.

~~~

It is useless to blame our unhappiness on someone who doesn't care, so we blame it on someone who does.

~~~

I had a dream. It was Judgment, and God said to me, "Before you blame your parents, I should tell you that they're already in heaven."

~~~

The trouble with having just one physical body is that so often you are mistaken for the previous occupant.

<><><>

<><><>

Ever wonder where you were on the day God gave everyone else their assignments?

~~~

One difference between good and evil is that evil never requires payments in the first year.

~~~

Ah, yes, good versus evil -- good offering the greater reward, evil the shorter wait.

~~~

A simple rule -- never let something that doesn't matter to you ruin something that does.

~~~

Most people who have an opinion about everything actually have just one opinion that applies to everything.

~~~

All I ask of anyone investigating my finances is to let me know if they find any.

~~~

<><><>

<><><>

Afterthoughts

It is wisest at times to do nothing and explain it by saying nothing.

~~~

If you reread Genesis, you find that the Creator looked around and saw that everything was good, not great.

~~~

You know you've run out of friends when it's down to you and your shadow, and a voice says, "You're in my light."

~~~

The poor still want to become rich, but it seems a distant memory when the ignorant wanted to become educated.

~~~

There are two parts to moving on in life -- living to tell about it and never speaking of it again.

~~~

There is a child in every one of us, not always accompanied by an adult.

<><><>

<> <> <>

I dunno -- seems like the only time you get an explanation these days is when a simple yes or no will do.

~~~

Have I ever been dealt a royal straight flush? Actually, yes -- happened in a game of Go Fish.

~~~

Folks who tell you, "Putting it off won't make it any easier," presume that there is some point where you plan to stop putting it off.

~~~

All I know about heaven and hell is that it's probably a mistake to judge them by the people who expect to go there.

~~~

It is possible to deny reality, especially if you avoid driving through certain parts of town.

~~~

Ah, yes, the highway "Text Stop." Formerly known as, "Rest Stop. No Facilities." Just the thing if you're starting to drip text into your pants.

<> <> <>